D1002197

IRISH DANCING

AND OTHER NATIONAL DANCES

RITA STOREY

SEA-TO-SEA

Mankato Collingwood London

IRISH DANCING
AND OTHER
NATIONAL DANCES

A national dance is a dance associated with a particular country. It is often a folk dance that has been adopted as a symbol of the country's culture and history—for example lively Irish dancing, passionate Spanish flamenco, or the beautiful and delicate dances of India.

National dances are often performed at important international events such as the opening of the Olympic Games. Because events like this are broadcast all over the world, the dances are seen by a huge audience. People become interested in learning the national dances of other countries. Irish dancing became very popular after it was shown during the 1994 Eurovision Song Contest, which was held in Dublin, in Ireland.

Why should *I* dance?

Dancing is good for everyone. It's a great way to get in shape. All types of dancing are a form of aerobic exercise, which encourages your heart and lungs to work hard. Over time, this will help them become stronger and get *you* in better shape.

The food we eat provides our body with the energy it needs to work properly. But if we eat more calories than our body needs, these are stored as fat. Dancing makes your body burn off calories. Your muscles will strengthen and become firmer, and your body will become more toned.

Dancing makes you happy

When you exercise, your brain makes a hormone called seratonin, which makes you feel happy. So if you're feeling miserable, put down the chocolate, put on the music, and get dancing.

There are so many types of dance there really is something for everyone. You can do the dance moves in this book on your own or with a friend, and work at a pace that suits you.

Dancing can even boost your brain power. Putting together dance steps increases your coordination and helps keep your mind alert.

Last but not least, dancing is fun. So what are you waiting for? Turn up the music and get moving!

Contents

Let's get moving

Why do I have to warm up?

Before you learn any new dance steps and begin to put them together, it is important to warm up your muscles so you don't get a cramp or strain a muscle. You may only be able to do the exercises a couple of times to start with, but don't give up. Just do a few more repeats each time. A warmup should last about ten minutes.

There are warmup moves in each of the four books in the *Get Dancing* series. You can combine them to make a routine.

Aerobic exercises

The first set of exercises is aerobic, which means it improves your breathing and circulation. Aerobic exercise increases your oxygen intake by making your heart beat faster. To do it, you have to keep on the move all the time. Each set of aerobic exercises is designed to be repeated. If you are not used to exercise and feel your pulse starting to race, stop and jog on the spot to keep warm.

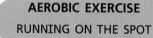

AEROBIC EXERCISE

RUNNING ON THE SPOT

1 Run on the spot. Start by running for 25 counts (count one when both feet have touched the floor). When that seems really easy, add another block of 25.

VARIATION
After running for a count of 50, do 5 jumps straight up in the air (keeping both feet together).

ISOLATION
SHOULDER

1. With your fingers resting on your shoulders, roll your shoulders forward, so that your elbows make a big circle.

2. With your fingers resting on your shoulders, roll your shoulders backward, so that your elbows make a big circle.

Repeat 4 times.

Body isolations

The second set of exercises is a body isolation. This type of exercise teaches you to move parts of your body individually, which is important for all types of dancing.

What to wear

Wear something comfortable to do a warmup, such as loose-fitting leggings (not jeans), a T-shirt, and a loose, long-sleeved top you can take off when you have warmed up.

You can do the routine in bare feet, sneakers, or jazz shoes. Don't do it in socks, or you may slip.

Dance to the music

You will need at least two pieces of music for the warmup. The first is for the aerobic exercises. It should be energetic and upbeat, to make everyone feel enthusiastic. It can also be used for body isolations, which are sharp, quick moves.

The second piece of music will be used for the stretches and toning exercises (see page 6). Gentle, relaxing music is best for this part of the warmup.

Let's get moving

Stretches

The most important thing to remember about stretches is that they should be done gradually. It's easy to pull a muscle by pushing yourself too hard, too soon.

Try doing the exercises every day and stretching just a little bit further each time. If it hurts, STOP. You may feel a little stiff the next day if you haven't been exercising regularly, but you shouldn't be in pain. If you are, you have stretched too hard. Stop for a few days and then slowly start building the stretches up again.

Toning exercises

These exercises strengthen and tone particular muscles, giving you a better body shape and strong muscles to hold the dance moves.

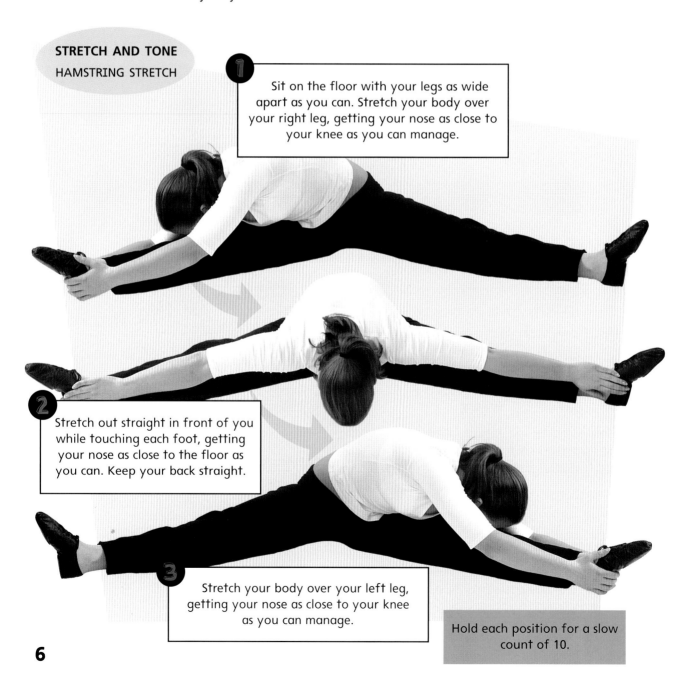

STRETCH AND TONE
HAMSTRING STRETCH

1 Sit on the floor with your legs as wide apart as you can. Stretch your body over your right leg, getting your nose as close to your knee as you can manage.

2 Stretch out straight in front of you while touching each foot, getting your nose as close to the floor as you can. Keep your back straight.

3 Stretch your body over your left leg, getting your nose as close to your knee as you can manage.

Hold each position for a slow count of 10.

6

Cool it!

At the end of a dance session, it is important to do a cool-down routine to help prevent stiffness the next day. The routine concentrates on stretching exercises that stretch out and relax the muscles. To be effective, each stretch should be held for a slow count of ten. A cool-down routine should last for five to ten minutes.

Hold each move for a slow count of 10.

Each of the four books in the *Get Dancing* series contains cool-down stretches. You can use a combination from different books if you wish.

COOL IT! 1
THIGH STRETCH

COOL IT! 2
ARM STRETCH

1 Standing with your feet together, bring your knee up to your chest and hug it tight.

2 Repeat with the other knee.

1 Stand with your feet apart. Interlock your fingers, and with your palms facing upward, stretch up your arms as high as you can.

Irish dancing

There are different kinds of Irish dancing: step dancing, ceili dancing, and set dancing.

Step dancing

Step dancing is a fast, high-kicking style of dancing performed as a solo dance or a group dance. It is danced with the arms held rigidly by the sides. Irish step dancers often enter competitions called feis (pronounced "fesh"). There are local, regional, national, and world feis. Step dances consist of jigs, reels, and hornpipes.

Ceili dancing

Ceili dancing (pronounced "kaylee") is Irish folk dancing. It is done in groups and the steps are easy to pick up. People dance it just for fun.

Set dancing

Set dancing is done in groups, using step-dancing moves.

A step-dancing dress worn for performing.

What to wear for step dancing

Practice clothes

Soft shoes (like ballet shoes) or hard tap shoes are worn.

Girls wear clothes that allow them to do high kicks: a short, full skirt or shorts. These are worn with a blouse with loose sleeves, or a T-shirt. Boys also wear a shirt with full sleeves or a T-shirt, and trousers or a kilt.

Performance clothes

For competitions, girls wear short, embroidered dresses. These are often made of heavy velvet and decorated with lots of Irish symbols. Girls often wear their hair in ringlets.

For some dances, soft shoes are worn. Girls' soft shoes are called gillies. These are like ballet shoes but with intricate lacing at the front. For other dances, hard shoes are needed. Girls' hard shoes have a metal plate on the heel and the toe.

Boys wear kilts or black pants, jackets, ties, vests, and hard or soft shoes.

RIVERDANCE

Stealing the show

In 1994, the Eurovision Song Contest was held in Dublin, Ireland. During a break between songs, a troupe of dancers performed a short step-dancing routine called "Riverdance." An audience of 300 million television viewers saw the beauty, grace, and excitement of Irish step dancing, and this ensured its future popularity.

The routine included traditional and modern music, and hard-shoe step dancing. The lead dancer, Michael Flatley, and Jean Butler, his female costar, gave an unforgettable performance. The audience was captivated. Some people thought it was the highlight of the Eurovision Song Contest.

Riverdance—the stage show

The response to the seven minutes of "Riverdance" was so positive that plans were made to create a stage show. In 1995, *Riverdance* opened as a two-hour show, with Michael Flatley and Jean Butler again dancing the lead roles.

Irish history

The *Riverdance* stage show explores Irish history through music, song, and dance. Most of the dancing is soft-shoe and hard-shoe Irish step dancing, but there are elements of Spanish, Russian, and African dance in it as well. These are there to reflect all the cultures that make up Ireland today.

The cast of the *Riverdance* stage show performing at the Apollo Theater, London.

Feet of flames

Basic steps in Irish step dancing

There are three basic types of step: threes, sevens, and jig steps.

Threes

The three-step can consist of jumps, hops, or kicks. It is used to dance in one place, or move forward or backward. To dance the jump threes step, you dance from your right foot to your left foot to your right foot. Then you dance from your left foot to your right foot to your left foot. Lift your knees high as you dance.

JUMP THREES

2 Kick your front (right) leg in the air, keeping it straight, with toes pointed.

1 Starting position: feet together, with the heel of the right foot by the toes of the left foot.

3 Jump off the back (left) foot onto the front (right) foot. As you do this, kick your back foot up and kick your bottom. As you land, put your back (left) foot down at the front. You should now be back in the basic position, but with the left foot in front.

HOP THREES

1 Starting position: feet together, with the heel of the right foot by the toes of the left foot. Hop (as high as you can) onto the back (left) foot. As you land on the left foot, bring your right foot up and across, as near to your left hipbone as you can manage.

2 Step onto the front (right) foot.

3 Put your left foot behind your right foot and you are back where you started. Repeat the sequence (in hop threes you don't change feet).

Feet of flames

Sevens

The seven step is a traveling step used when you want to dance to the side. When dancing sevens, you are moving in the direction of the foot that is in front. The front foot stays in front.

SEVENS

MOVING TO THE LEFT

1 Starting position: feet together, with the heel of the left foot by the toes of the right foot.
Hop on the back (right) foot. Bring your left foot up as high as you can toward your hipbone (see page 11). You won't be able to do this immediately. Start by bringing your foot up to knee height and try to get it a bit higher each time you practice.

2 Jump onto your front (left) foot, placing it in front and to the left of the right foot.

3 Cross your back (right) foot behind your left foot, and hop onto it.

Body positions for Irish step dancing

When step dancing, always remember to keep your arms straight by your sides. Your hands should be closed into a fist, with your thumb tucked inside.

Keep your head up, with your neck straight and your shoulders back.

Keep your feet in a pointed position. Never turn up your toes so that you show the sole of your foot. Lift your knees high as you dance.

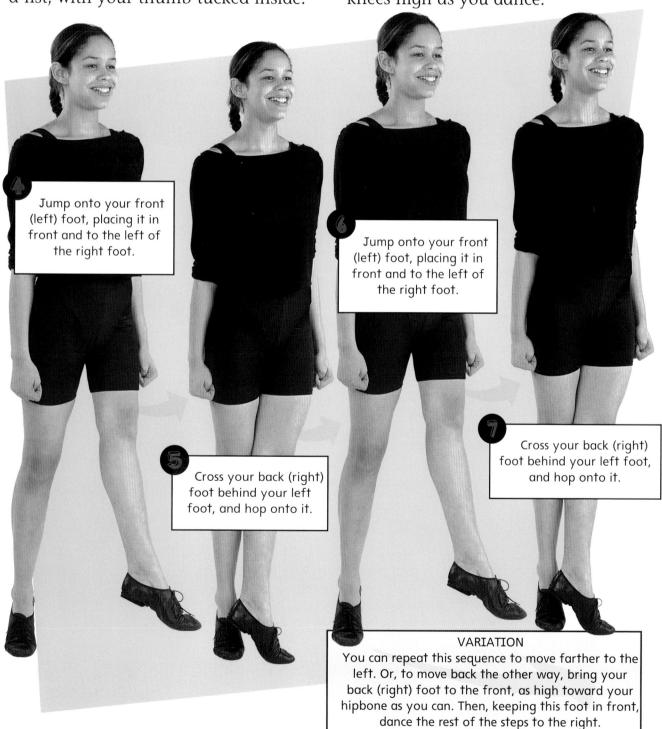

4 Jump onto your front (left) foot, placing it in front and to the left of the right foot.

5 Cross your back (right) foot behind your left foot, and hop onto it.

6 Jump onto your front (left) foot, placing it in front and to the left of the right foot.

7 Cross your back (right) foot behind your left foot, and hop onto it.

VARIATION
You can repeat this sequence to move farther to the left. Or, to move back the other way, bring your back (right) foot to the front, as high toward your hipbone as you can. Then, keeping this foot in front, dance the rest of the steps to the right.

Feet of flames

Jig step

This jig step is a traveling step, where you move forward and change feet. It combines the jump threes and the hop threes described on pages 10–11.

JIG STEP

1. Starting position: feet together, with the heel of the left foot by the toes of the right foot.
Hop on the back (right) foot. Bring your left foot up as high as you can toward your hipbone (see page 11). You won't be able to do this immediately. Start by bringing your foot up to knee height and try to get it a bit higher each time you practice.

2. Jump onto your front (left) foot, placing it in front and to the left of the right foot.

3. Cross your back (right) foot behind your front (left) foot, and hop onto it.

Dance to the music

Riverdance (composer Bill Whelan). *Lord of The Dance* (composer Ronan Hardiman). *Feet of Flames* (composer Ronan Hardiman). Mike Shaffer: *Dance to the Music—Traditional Irish Dance Music*. Pat King: *Three Score and Ten*.

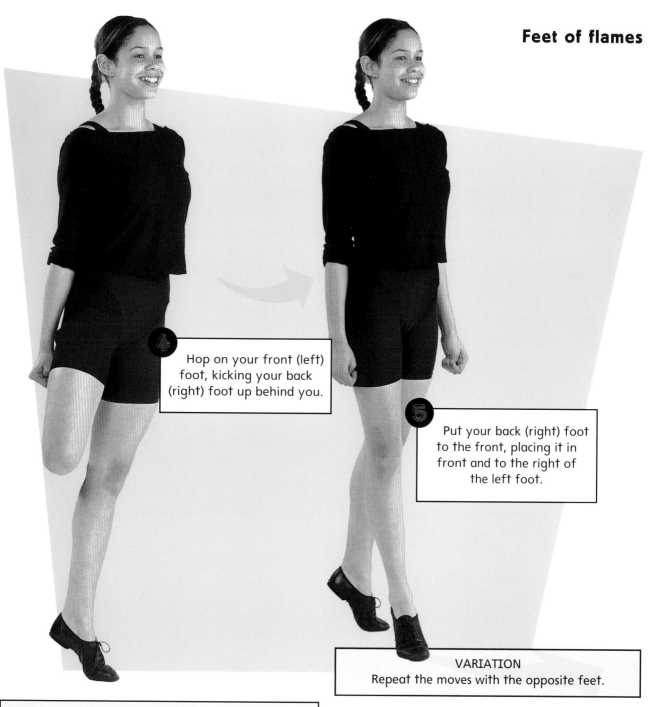

4 Hop on your front (left) foot, kicking your back (right) foot up behind you.

5 Put your back (right) foot to the front, placing it in front and to the right of the left foot.

VARIATION
Repeat the moves with the opposite feet.

VARIATION
Once you've done the jig step, try combining some of the basic steps. Do jump threes twice, then sevens to the right, sevens to the left, and hop threes twice. Repeat from the beginning.

Skilled dancers

Experienced Irish step dancers have a special way of changing their weight from one side of the body to the other (shown right). Don't try it yourself. It takes a lot of practice to be able to perform it without hurting your feet.

Spanish flamenco

The flamenco rhythm

Spanish flamenco dancing is danced to an uneven, twelve-beat rhythm. This can make it difficult to dance, because most of the dances we are used to are danced to a regular beat. The rhythm of flamenco is counted with the emphasis on the third, sixth, eighth, tenth, and twelfth beat.

1 2 **3** 4 5 **6** 7 **8** 9 **10** 11 **12**

Counting the rhythm

Count out loud from one to twelve. Say the numbers **3**, **6**, **8**, **10**, and **12** louder than the rest. Can you hear the rhythm?

Clapping the rhythm

Now clap your hands while you count. Clap harder on beats **3**, **6**, **8**, **10**, and **12**.

Stamping the rhythm

First stamp your left foot and then your right foot, twelve times, stamping harder on beats **3**, **6**, **8**, **10**, and **12**.

Dancing the rhythm

Now count the beats one to twelve in your head and stamp and clap at the same time, stamping and clapping louder on beats **3**, **6**, **8**, **10**, and **12**.

Hold your hands up high as you clap. Can you feel yourself flamenco dancing already?

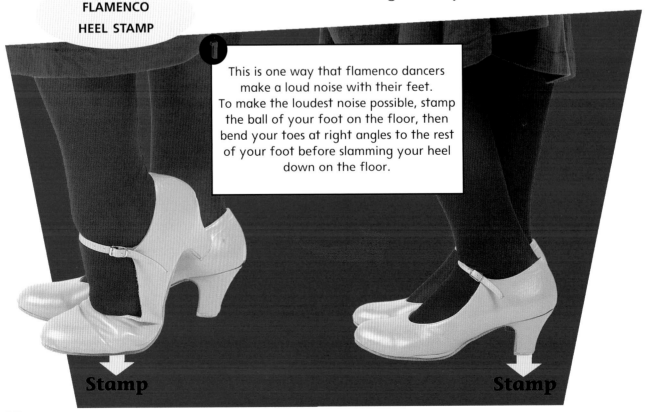

FLAMENCO HEEL STAMP

This is one way that flamenco dancers make a loud noise with their feet. To make the loudest noise possible, stamp the ball of your foot on the floor, then bend your toes at right angles to the rest of your foot before slamming your heel down on the floor.

Stamp   **Stamp**

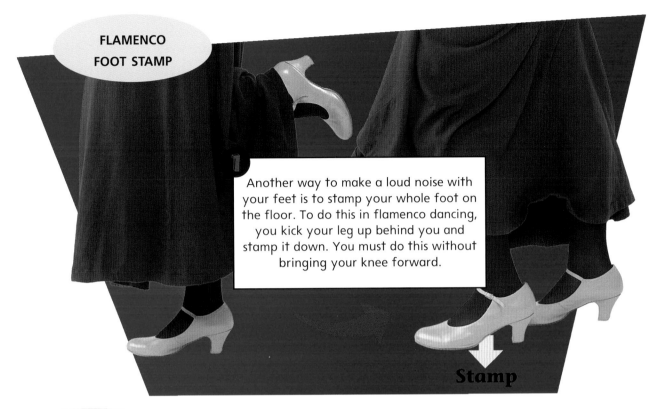

FLAMENCO
FOOT STAMP

Another way to make a loud noise with your feet is to stamp your whole foot on the floor. To do this in flamenco dancing, you kick your leg up behind you and stamp it down. You must do this without bringing your knee forward.

Stamp

FLAMENCO
HAND CLAPPING

Standing tall

It is important to stand correctly before you begin. Your shoulders should be relaxed and pulled back, your back straight, and your head held high. Your knees should be slightly bent and your weight should all be in the lower half of your body. This feels strange at first, but as you start to tap and stamp your feet, it becomes quite natural.

Hand clapping

The Spanish word for the hand clapping in flamenco is *"palmas."* Palmas is either loud or soft.

To clap loudly, hold your left hand up to head height, cup the palm, and hit it with the middle three fingers of your right hand. When this is done correctly, it makes a sharp, loud clap. To clap softly, cup the fingers of both hands and clap them together to make a gentler sound.

17

Spanish flamenco

Arms and hands

One of the most characteristic things about flamenco dancing is the way that the girls use their arms. The arms are held up high, in a gentle curve, so that the elbows do not stick out. The hands are then turned from the wrist to make the dance movements.

FLAMENCO STEP SEQUENCE

Stamp

Stamp

Stamp

1 Starting position: feet together, arms at waist height, crossed at the wrists with the palms facing up.
Stamp with the right foot, counting the beats as you do so. Stamp first with the ball of your foot (on count 1), then heel (on count 2), then the whole foot (on count 3).
As you make each move, gradually bring your arms up higher.
1 2 **3**

2 Stamp the ball of your left foot (on count 4).
4

3

Stamp the heel of your left foot
(on count 5).
Stamp the whole left foot (on count 6).
5 **6**

4

Your arms should now be up
alongside your head.
Stamp your right foot, then your left
foot, clapping as you stamp: clap and
stamp six times, stamping louder on beats
8, 10, and 12.
7 **8** 9 **10** 11 **12**

Stamp

Stamp

Stamp

Stamp

Dance to the music

Various artists: *Fire &
Passion: The New Flamenco.*
Paco Peña: *Fabulous
Flamenco.* Various artists: *The Rough
Guide to Flamenco.*

VARIATION
This sequence may seem very simple, but the
flamenco tempo is very fast. Start slowly and then
speed up. Roll your hands over each other, keeping
your wrists together.

What to wear

Practice clothes

Girls require flamenco shoes, which are made of suede or leather, with a heel of 1–2 inches. (3–5 cm) high. They have little pieces of metal on the heel and toes, for tapping out the rhythms of the dance. Or, tap shoes can be worn.

Girls also need a practice skirt. This should be long, and either plain or with ruffles. It is worn with an undershirt called a maillot (a close-fitting T-shirt would be a good substitute).

Boys wear plain slacks and a T-shirt. They also wear shoes with metal on the heel and toe.

Performance clothes

For dancing at festivals, girls wear a traditional flamenco dress. This is long, with ruffles on the skirt and sleeves. Large colored flowers are pinned in the hair, which is usually worn in a bun.

For dancing on stage, the style of dress is simpler, using flowing shapes rather than ruffles.

Traditionally, boys used to wear high-waisted slacks, shirts with frills, and a short jacket with a sash. That has now changed and modern flamenco dancers wear plain slacks and a shirt in a dark color.

Accessories

Expert flamenco dancers use props to perform some of their dances. These include a shawl (*manton*), a fan (*pericon*), and castanets (*castañuelas*). Castanets are wooden disks clicked together in time to the music.

A famous modern flamenco dancer, Joaquim Cortes, dancing in his show *Soul*. Many flamenco dance performances today are done in simple costumes that make it easy to see the movements of the body.

THE SPIRIT OF FLAMENCO

Gypsy dance

Flamenco is the most famous of Spain's traditional dances. It was invented by gypsies (*flamencos*) in Andalusia in southern Spain. This type of dancing is performed on a hard floor, with hard shoes, and is very rhythmic.

Flamenco style

Flamenco is made up of three things: song (*canto*), dance (*baile*), and guitar-playing (*guitarra*). Men and women dance different steps. Men do intricate toe-and-heel-clicking steps, while the women's dance has more graceful hand and body movements.

Music

Flamenco dances are traditionally accompanied by Spanish guitar and a pair of castanets, which the dancers often play themselves. The dances also involve clapping, foot stamping, and shouting to the beat of the music.

There are dozens of different forms of flamenco, and within each form there are many variations. Different areas of Spain have their own particular styles of the dance.

Expressing feelings

As well as basic steps, flamenco dancing involves improvisation. Each dancer uses the dance to express his or her feelings about things such as love, hate, pride, sorrow, and joy. A really good flamenco dancer has what the Spanish call "*duende*" (pronounced "dwen-day"), a special inner feeling that inspires the dancer to great performances.

Fiestas

In Spain, people enjoy big outdoor parties called fiestas. In Seville there is a huge fiesta every spring, which goes on all day and all night. A million people take part in the fun. All around Seville, tents of brightly colored canvas are set up to use as dance halls. There is music and flamenco dancing, and everyone is encouraged to join in. Many of the women wear colorful gypsy flamenco dresses.

To dance flamenco, you need to stand very upright and look proud and confident.

Indian dancing

Indian dancing is very complicated. As well as learning the steps, you also need to learn the correct rhythms and postures. Indian dance is a blend of three things: *nritta, nrity,* and *natya.*

Nritta is the body movements made to the rhythms of a dance.

Nrity is the combination of rhythm and expression. It is shown through the eyes, hands, and facial expression.

Natya is the storytelling element of a dance, when the dance is used to depict an Indian legend.

Bharata natyam

One classical form of Indian dancing is bharata natyam, which is traditionally danced by women.

Before each session, the dancer recites a prayer to the Earth to apologize for stamping on the ground, because the dances involve beating a rhythm on the ground with bare feet.

Traditionally, bharata natyam takes seven years to learn because it is so complicated. It has 120 basic steps called *adavus,* made up of poses and movements. Some are shown on pages 22 to 26 for you to try out and perhaps use in your own dances.

This is one of a group of bharata natyam adavus called nattadavu, which are stretching movements.

NATTADAVU **1**

CLASSICAL INDIAN DANCING

Classical Indian dances are among the most graceful in the world. Learning them is like learning a new language. Combinations of movements of the feet, knees, hips, arms, legs, hands, head, and eyes can mean many different things.

There are six major classical dances, each of which developed in a different region of India. They were all originally devotional dances to various gods. The six dances are:

kathakali and mohiniyattam,
bharata natyam,
kuchipudi,
odissi,
manipuri,
kathak.

Two of these classical styles—kathak and bharata natyam—are still very popuar today.

Kathak
Kathak comes from northern India. This style of dance tells a story. Originally, it was danced by people called kathakas, who told stories from history while entertaining people with dance, mime, and music. Kathak involves fast, whirling movements.

Bharata natyam
This style of dance comes from southern India. "Bharata" is made up of three words, which stand for emotion, melody, and rhythm. "Natyam" means the art of dance.

The 120 adavus (basic steps) in bharata natyam split into two types: poses (*sthanakas*) and movements (*charis*). These elements must be learned before any actual dancing starts. Then they are combined into groups of steps (*jethis*), then sequences (*thirmanams*), and finally into whole dances.

The hand movements in bharata natyam have special meanings.

Indian dancing

Sarikkal adavus are a series of sliding moves with the feet ("*sarikkal*" means "to slide") combined with intricate arm and hand movements.

Mai adavus are moves that use the flexibility of the whole body ("*mai*" means "body").

SARIKKAL ADAVU

The nine emotions

In Indian dancing, you learn to display nine emotions or *navrasas*, which are expressed by the eyes, the face, and the body, and are common to all classical Indian dance. The emotions are: happiness (*hasya*), anger (*krodha*), disgust (*bhibasta*), fear (*bhaya*), sorrow (*shoka*), courage (*viram*), wonder (*adbhuta*), serenity (*shanta*), and compassion (*karuna*).

East meets West

You might like to try blending some of the adavus with modern Western dance steps to create an exciting and original dance routine, just like they do in Bollywood movies (see page 27). Combine lots of influences, such as hip-hop dance steps and modern tap.

MAI ADAVU

What to wear

Hindu temple dancers

The dances of bharata natyam have a long history.

Originally they would have been danced by women who dedicated their lives to the Hindu religion and were considered to be married to the gods. They were called the handmaids of the gods, or *devadasis*. The devadasis would dance in the temples as part of religious ceremonies.

Costume

The history of bharata natyam is reflected in the outfits worn by girls who dance it today. They wear a costume designed to resemble a Hindu temple sculpture. These sculptures are frequently decorated with flowers and ornaments, so the costumes often include flowers and jewelry.

A dancer wearing a traditional bharata natyam costume.

Clothes to move in

The costume may be a dress, or a top and a pair of loose leggings. Dresses are pleated at the front to allow ease of movement. If leggings are worn, a pleated section called a *pallu* is attached to the front.

Feet

The dances are performed in bare feet. Dancers often decorate their feet by painting on intricate designs with a dye called henna. Anklets with rows of bells are worn to add a musical accompaniment to the moves.

Indian dancing

One group of adavus is called nattadavu (see also page 22). These are stretching movements. In the adavu shown here, the left leg is stretched out, with the heel striking the floor. The foot is then brought back alongside the right foot and stamped. The movement is repeated with the right leg.

Dance to the music

Cultural Center of India: *Dances of India—Bharata Natyam Songs*. Various artists: *The Best of Bollywood*. The orginal London cast of *Bombay Dreams—Bombay Dreams*.

NATTADAVU 2

BOLLYWOOD

Many people have come to know classical Indian dance because of the popularity of Indian musical movies all around the world.

The Indian movie industry is one of the biggest in the world, and many of the movies are an exciting and colorful mix of music, dancing, songs, and comedy. The movies blend different classical Indian dance styles with Western dance steps.

Bollywood movies

Most Indian movies are made in the city of Mumbai, which has been nicknamed Bollywood. This is a combination of the words "Hollywood" and "Bombay" (the old name for Mumbai).

Bollywood movies have made people much more aware of Indian dance. Classes in kathak and bharata natyam are becoming very popular in many countries.

Bombay Dreams

In 2002, a stage musical called *Bombay Dreams* opened in London. The musical was produced by Andrew Lloyd Webber. He created a Bollywood-style show full of songs and dance routines, using a cast of Asian performers.

Dancers in the Bollywood movie *Kisna*.

Other national dances

National dances help give people a sense of belonging. Sometimes, countries go through difficult times. If a country is occupied by people with a different cultural background as a result of war, the traditions of the resident population may be suppressed. At times like this in particular, traditional songs and dances help people remember their own culture and identity.

The samba

The Brazilians hold a huge festival in spring, called carnival. It is one of the biggest festivals in the world today. In Brazil's largest city, Rio de Janeiro, the streets come alive with people dressed in exotic costumes dancing the samba.

Carnival was originally a religious festival people celebrated before fasting for forty days over Lent.

The samba comes from African culture. The dance became part of carnival in the early 1900s when a large number of black Brazilians moved to the slums of Rio after the abolition of slavery in Brazil.

The haka

The haka is a Maori war dance from New Zealand. It was performed to get warriors into top physical condition to fight a battle.

Today, the haka has been adopted as a pregame battle dance by the All Blacks, New Zealand's national rugby team (see page 30 for details of a website that tells you how to do it).

During the haka, the men contort their face, roll their eyes, and cry, *"Ka Mate! Ka Mate!"* This is designed to unsettle their opponents and ensure a victory.

Not all haka dances were war dances. Some were used to welcome and entertain visitors.

Roll your eyes, waggle your tongue, and look fierce to dance the haka.

Belly dancing

This ancient dance originated in the Middle East. Its proper name is *raks sharqui*, meaning "dance of the East." In belly dancing, the hips are actually used more than the belly. The head, shoulders, and arms are also used. Some people believe that belly dancing was a form of goddess worship. It is still used as a healing dance in parts of North Africa.

Dragon dance

The dragon dance is an important tradition in China. In Chinese culture, the dragon is a rain god, and the dance was originally performed to bring an end to a drought.

This dance is now performed at various festivals, but more as entertainment than for any religious or spiritual purpose.

A colorful dragon is made out of paper stretched over a frame. It has poles attached to the underside, which the performers hold. A dragon can be up to 328 feet (100 meters) long. The performers dance along, raising and lowering the dragon with the poles so that it looks as though it is leaping and diving through the crowd.

Highland dancing

In Scotland, men traditionally took part in special dances as a test of their strength, agility, and stamina. These dances were performed at the Highland Games, and were also used by Scottish soldiers as a type of fitness training.

The oldest of the highland dances is the highland fling. This is a dance of celebration, performed after a victory in battle. It is danced over a pair of crossed swords, which may originally have been the sword of the victor and of his defeated adversary.

Belly dancing costumes are heavily embroidered and often have jewels sewn on them. Simple copies can be rented from costume suppliers.

Further information

Websites

wikipedia.org
Search "Indian classical dance" and you will find a picture showing lots of different bharata natyam moves being danced.

www.riverdance.com
There are some good video and audio clips on this site.

www.newzealand.com
Learn the moves and words for the traditional haka dance performed by the All Blacks rugby team before an international game.

DVDs, videos, and CDs

Irish Dancing Step by Step, Volume I, Olive Hurley
A video that teaches five soft-shoe dances: easy reel, easy jig, easy slip-jig, easy single jig, walls of Limerick.

Irish Dancing Step by Step, Volume 2, Olive Hurley
A video that teaches five hard-shoe dances: treble jig, hornpipe and the traditional set dances, St. Patrick's Day dance, the blackbird.

Manuel Salado—El Baile Flamenco
A collection of DVDs and CDs that introduces the basics of flamenco dancing. For beginners and more experienced dancers.

Dances of India—Learning Bharata Natyam
This DVD includes: salutation, basic positions, hand gestures, warmup exercises, head movements, eye movements, and poses, as well as costumes and makeup.

Note to parents and teachers: every effort has been made by the Publishers to ensure these websites are suitable for children, are of the highest educational value, and contain no inappropriate or offensive material. Because of the nature of the Internet, however, it is impossible to guarantee that the contents of these sites will not be altered. We strongly advise that Internet access is supervised by a responsible adult.

Dancing is a fun way to get in shape but like any form of physical exercise it has an element of risk, particularly if you are unfit, overweight, or suffer from any medical conditions. It is advisable to consult a healthcare professional before beginning any program of exercise.

Glossary

Adavus The 120 basic steps (movements and poses) of the Indian classical dance bharata natyam.

Aerobic exercise Exercise that improves breathing and circulation.

Baile The element of dance in Spanish flamenco.

Beat The regular pulse in a piece of music. In flamenco dancing, the beat is irregular (see page 16).

Bharata natyam A type of Indian classical dance.

Bollywood A nickname for Mumbai in India, where many Indian musical movies are made.

Canto Spanish flamenco singing.

Castanets Wooden disks that are held in the hand and clicked together in time to Spanish flamenco music.

Ceili (pronounced "kaylee") Irish folk dancing.

Coordination The ability to move different parts of the body together at the same time.

Duende A special inner feeling that inspires flamenco dancers to great performances.

Feis (pronounced "fesh") Competitions for Irish step dancers.

Fiesta An outdoor party in Spain.

Flamenco A type of rhythmic and passionate dance that originated in Andalusia in Spain. It is danced on a hard floor, with hard shoes, and involves stamping and clapping.

Gillies Soft shoes with intricate lacing, worn by girls for Irish step dancing.

Guitarra Spanish flamenco guitar-playing.

Haka A Maori dance. Today it is performed by the New Zealand rugby team before international games.

Hormone A substance produced by the body that affects the way the body functions.

Improvisation Making up steps as you dance.

Isolations A type of exercise involving moving one part of the body without moving the rest.

Kathak An Indian classical dance.

Palmas Hand clapping in Spanish flamenco dancing.

Rhythm The regular sounds in a piece of music.

Ruffles The gathered pieces of material that decorate traditional flamenco dresses.

Index

This edition first published in 2007 by
Sea-to-Sea Publications
1980 Lookout Drive,
North Mankato
Minnesota 56003

Copyright © Sea-to-Sea Publications 2007

Library of Congress Cataloging in Publication Data
Storey, Rita.
  Irish dancing / by Rita Storey.
    p.cm. -- (Get dancing)
  Includes bibliographical references (p.) and index.
  ISBN *978-1-59771-050-3
    1. Dance--Ireland--Juvenile literature. 2, Folk dancing, Irish--Juvenile literature.
  I.Title. II. Series.

GV1646.I8S76 2006
793.3'19415 – dc22

2005058150

9 8 7 6 5 4 3 2

Published by arrangement with the Watts Publishing Group Ltd., London

Series editor: Rachel Cooke
Art director: Peter Scoulding

Series designed and created for Franklin Watts by STOREYBOOKS Ltd.

Designer: Rita Storey
Editor: Fiona Corbridge
Photography: Tudor Photography, Banbury
Dance consultant: Lucie-Grace Welsman

Picture credits
Corbis/ Robbie Jack p.9; Corbis Sygma/ Beirne Brendan p.21; Corbis/ Reuters/ Arko Datta p.27.

Cover images: Tudor Photography, Banbury, UK.

All photos posed by models.
Thanks to James Boyce, Kimesha Campbell, Hazel Hathway, Ricky Healey, Aisha Hussain, Fern Jelleyman, Charlie Storey, and Hannah Storey.

With many thanks to Goody Two Shoes, Rugby, UK, who supplied all the costumes.